An unexpected MIRACLE

Conquering Brain Injury

Jennifer De Pippo

with

Bennett R. Coles

PROMONTORY
PRESS

All rights reserved. No part of this publication may be reproduced, stored in a retrieval system, or transmitted, in any form or by any means, electronic, mechanical, photocopying, recording, or otherwise, without the written prior permission of the publisher.

An unexpected MIRACLE

Copyright © 2014 by Jennifer De Pippo

Promontory Press
www.promontorypress.com

First Edition: May 2014

ISBN 978-1-927559-07-9

Cover and interior design by SpicaBookDesign.
Printed in Canada
0 9 8 7 6 5 4 3 2 1

An unexpected MIRACLE

Conquering Brain Injury

Jennifer De Pippo

Acknowledgements

My sincere gratitude goes out not only to the people who helped me write this book but also to the ones that have helped me progress through my journey.

To my dad, who has not only raised me and provided for me, but who has also been a loving father, mentor, and coach. You have always been there for me during happy times and sad. I am truly grateful to have a dad like you.

To my sister who helped me understand my womanhood. I couldn't rely on my dad to explain changes that were happening to my body. I am truly grateful.

To the *Societe de l'assurance automobile de Quebec (SAAQ)* for providing me with a copy of my lengthy medical file. The information helped me write my story; it gave me the facts.

To the neurosurgeons who did a tremendous job on my operation. Your work shines in the progress I make every day.

To the many therapists I worked with over the years, who helped me reestablish myself mentally, physically, emotionally, and spiritually. You are miracle workers.

To my school teachers for having patience with me and providing lectures for me outside of class time. Thank you for helping me reach my educational goals.

To Bill and Sandra Roberts, who encouraged me to publish my story. You helped me realize that I'd made big accomplishments over the years that I should be proud of. Thank you to Bill for being patient and encouraging me in everything I do. There aren't enough words to express my sincere appreciation of the interest you took in making me succeed. Thank you to Sandra for having interesting conversations with me and helping me expand my mind. I am proud to call you my friends.

To the friendly staff at Fitness Incorporated in Cranbrook, BC. You've provided me with a clean and comfortable space where I can continue my daily exercises. It is crucial that I continue to move my body to prevent the loss of what I have already accomplished. Thank you.

To the many editors, graphic designers and publishers who have helped make my book a success. Thank you for your hard work.

To my neighbors and acquaintances who have encouraged and supported me through my tough endeavors. Thank you.

I would like to also acknowledge the website Neuroskills.com for providing me with important and helpful information in writing my book. Thank you.

Foreword

"Are you afraid of me?"

That was the question offered up to me by a young woman named Jennifer. It was a question that certainly made me step back and reassess how I viewed the handicapped.

For much too long, people have viewed handicapped people with indifference, a lack of respect and a pretence of sympathy. I'm sure that those with a handicap have experienced it all and suffer quietly, as we expect them to. We have no time for, and seldom show, empathy for complaining.

But this young woman was not going away until she had my answer. Jennifer and I got off to a rocky start because of the presumption that I had made when I first met her. She straightened me out about her handicap, quite powerfully, in fact.

"No, I'm not afraid of you," I replied, and so started a friendship between a seventy year-old retired miner and one of the most courageous people I have ever met.

I first noticed Jennifer in the gym where we both work out, and what I saw was a very lonely and sad individual. It's amazing how a simple "Hi, how are you today?" can make a difference to a handicapped person. Most of them are not used to being acknowledged and the smile they return is worth its weight in gold.

Over time, Jennifer and I got to know each other and became good friends. I encouraged her to specifically work on the side of her body that was injured in a horrific car accident. Over time, I could see the change in her body, but more importantly, I could see the growth in confidence in her own ability.

As I helped her, she taught me and gave me insight to what the handicapped have to go through daily; a world of rejection, intolerance and, the largest issue, a complete lack of understanding from others.

A member of my own family experienced a similar accident and injury to that of Jennifer and her family, so I know how those around someone that has endured such a trauma expect them to act as if they are cured and back to normal. Of course, that isn't ever going to happen. Brain damage is life-altering for both the person involved and all of those around them.

Over the months, Jennifer's transformation was quite noticeable to those in the gym. She evolved from a shy person seeking acceptance as a fellow human being, into a bold and strong woman. As you get to know her you will find that she is a very beautiful and intelligent person.

'Patience' is what I take out of our friendship. I now have a healthy respect for a person that has shown resilience to the slings and arrows cast at her and others in her situation. Jennifer is a teacher in her own way and she is my friend. She would make anyone proud to call her their daughter.

Listen to Jennifer as she tells her story. It is an eye opener.

"There, but for the grace of God, go I." It could have been me.

Bill Roberts

Author, *The Best Miners in the World*

Preface

Life before the accident

I am not a best-selling author like Danielle Steel or Nicholas Sparks. I have not risen to fame through a video posted on YouTube like Justin Beiber. I am not like Michael J. Fox, Rick Hansen, or Terry Fox who have left their footprints in society by creating a Foundation in honor of themselves. I am just an ordinary person with an extraordinary story of survival to tell.

My intent for this book is to inspire at least one person who is suffering from a traumatic injury. I hope that they can realize that the light of life can shine for them too: all it takes is a positive attitude and the realization that the light takes time to shine. I suffered a brain injury and I had to endure 18 years before the light really began to shine on me. For those of you who are just reading my book out of curiosity, I hope to enlighten you with my story.

People who suffer traumatic injuries don't need pity: we need respect. Respect for our determination to keep on living despite the challenges, to accomplish what the average person takes for granted, but which to us are triumphs.

I was born in Montreal's Jewish General Hospital on June 28, 1987 at 2:36 in the morning to two loving Italian parents. I was delivered by obstetrician/gynecologist Dr. Janet Schinder. I weighed six pounds, one ounce when I came out of my mother's womb with light brown hair and blue eyes (they eventually turned hazel). I measured in at 21 inches long – definitely a keeper!

I was apparently the perfect baby… I ate and slept. I didn't fuss too much. I could sleep with any kind of noise, whether the television was on full blast or my parents were talking with great animation to their company. When I was tired, I slept. When I was offered food, I ate it.

My early years were pretty typical. My big sister is three years older than me and loved having me around. But with the usual fun and games came the usual bumps and bruises. I clearly remember the night I had to be rushed to the hospital. I was about 12 months old and I had begun to crawl. My sister wanted to play doggy with me; I naturally played the dog. Somehow she scared me and I accidentally hit my forehead on the edge of the marble steps. Our playtime was cut short as I was rushed to the hospital immediately to get seven stitches on my lower forehead. But I was ready the next day to get right back to playing. I was anything but a fragile little princess!

Living in the beautiful city of Montreal, there were plenty of attractions such as La Ronde (an amusement park), Botanical Gardens and the Insectarium to keep me fascinated as a child. We lived in Little Italy, a small part of Montreal's distinctive culture and history. Even though the city's official language was French, it was very open and multicultural. The summer months were usually hot and humid; your skin felt wet and sticky, the weight of the air made you want to fall asleep. Whoever invented air conditioners was probably thinking of those poor Quebecois. The winter months, however, were brutally cold with heavy snowfalls, but we just bundled up under thick layers and played outside until dark.

My grandmother still talks about the delicious apple pies my mom made in those days. My neighbors would come over as soon as she pulled one out of the oven. Mom's pies were so good that the pie plate was clean within minutes. If you wanted a piece you had to be quick.

My sister started school three years before me and her smarts were clearly visible. *Gee,* I thought, *when I go to school I want to be just as smart as her.* Well, having loved daycare I was totally ready when it was finally my turn to start school, and I was just as smart. I liked going to school. Learning was fun. My smarts came naturally. In the second grade I even received several awards in recognition of my hard work.

My mom really got involved in my school community. She was always the first to volunteer for any activity, whether it was a class field trip or organizing the school year book. I remember when I was in Grade 2 my English teacher asked my mom if she could bake a cake in the mold of a teddy bear for a surprise teddy bear party. I could just hear Mom's enthusiastic response, "I would love to!" She always put my sister and I first. She helped us with our homework (maybe that's why I'm so smart!) and encouraged us in extra-curricular activities.

The year I finished second grade is when my life changed…

Chapter 1

When life takes a wrong turn...

On June 25, 1995, three days before my eighth birthday, to mark the end of another school year and the beginning of summer holidays, my mom, dad, sister, and I got into the car and drove to my aunt's and uncle's country cottage in Ste-Jerome, Quebec. The cottage was wonderful. The backyard was surrounded by tall trees for maximum privacy and the front was picturesque with neatly-cut grass and flowers that were beautifully manicured. We had come to the cottage for the day to escape the chaos of the city; to kick back, relax, and enjoy the beautiful June sun.

Then, on the drive home, our lives changed forever. It had been another great day and I was nestled contently in the back seat, the heavy summer heat and gentle rumble of the car lulling me to sleep. Then something ahead of the car forced my dad to swerve violently. We spun off the roadway and slid helplessly on the unfinished gravel of a roadside construction site. The car smashed in a heavy-duty forklift on the front passenger side, where my mom was sitting. A fork pierced through the passenger window and my mom's neck. That is how I lost her.

As for me, the impact of the crash meant my brain took a huge blow in my **cranium** (skull), which injured my **frontal lobe** and **cerebellum**. I suffered a **contrecoup** brain injury. My brain was "knocked" between the walls of my skull, severing the left hemisphere but causing damage throughout.

Within minutes the police, firefighters, paramedics, and news reporters arrived at the scene of the accident. I was rushed to a rural hospital in Ste. Jerome, Quebec. Immediately after being stabilized, I was transported to a bigger hospital in the city of Montreal called Sainte Justine. A CT scan

an unexpected MIRACLE

revealed a fracture on the left side of my frontal cranium 13mm deep—almost half an inch. My brain suffered from **intracranial pressure**, so **neurosurgeons** had no choice but to operate on me immediately. (These were no ordinary doctors: they were the most experienced, highly skilled neurosurgeons.) I also experienced **intracerebral hematoma** (internal bleeding) in my brain and a bruise on my abdomen.

Neurosurgeons started operating on me at 12:35am and finished at 3:00pm. Those fourteen hours in the O.R. must have seemed like an eternity at the time, but they were a blink of an eye compared to the entire life they've given me since. The operation was made up of three components: re-inverting my cranium back into place, drilling a hole on the left side of my head to relieve the **intracranial pressure**, and covering the hole with plasticity. To perform surgery on my cranium, my head was shaved about half way down.

Neurosurgeons then cut the skin of my scalp, from the top of my right ear to the top of my left ear to gain full access to my cranium. (Luckily I was on **general anesthesia** during the operation so I didn't feel anything. I wasn't even aware of what was happening.) After re-inverting my cranium, the rest of my brain was examined for any further wounds. Then, my scalp was stitched back together.

Once everything was completed, I was induced into a **coma**. This is standard procedure after such a traumatic operation, as the body needs a chance to heal from its many wounds, but it was probably one of the scariest things I've ever experienced. I didn't know where I was. I thought I had died. I was so scared I wanted to think it was all a bad dream. After the operation I was taken to the intensive care unit, where I spent the next two months.

I was in such a critical condition that for 16 days I laid in a glass tube. The glass tube isolated me from the world beyond and prevented me from

an unexpected MIRACLE

catching any other germs. There were wires attached to me from head to toe; I looked like a tree with too many branches. The wires were crucial for my body to heal. One of the wires was a feeding tube. It was inserted through my nostrils and extended down into my stomach. When the nurses pushed the tube up my nostrils I had become responsive (also known as **stupor**) for a split second due to the feeling of excruciating pain. For those 16 days, I was hooked up to so many machines that a nurse had to sit beside me 24 hours a day. The doctors encouraged my dad to talk to me or play music because they thought it might help with my recovery.

"Talk to your daughter. She is still here with her mind," the doctor told my dad.

Three days later, June 28 1995, was my eighth birthday. My dad sang "Happy Birthday" to me while I was lying in my coma.

Jennifer De Pippo

No one knew if I was ever going to recover. The **neurologists** measured my **Glasgow coma score** (the number that measures responsiveness in a coma) to be 6. This number can be classified as having a severe brain injury with minimal responsiveness. The Glasgow Coma Score (GCS) is scored between 3 and 15; the lower the score, the more severe the brain injury. Three distinct parameters are used to derive this score: Best Eye Response, Best Verbal Response, and Best Motor Response. A GCS of 13 or higher correlates with a mild brain injury, 9 to 12 is considered a moderate brain injury, and 8 or less is considered a severe brain injury.

Soon enough the whole Italian community in Montreal heard about what happened and showed their sympathy to my dad. Italians stick close together. All the people in my extended family were heartbroken, especially the ones that were closest to

an unexpected MIRACLE

my mom. My grandparents grieved the loss of their daughter.

Mom was 37 years old when she passed. Her grave can be found in the mausoleum in Laval, Quebec. The slab of marble on the front reads "De Pippo Michelina Polletta, 10-10-1957 to 25-6-1995." Above the writing there is a picture of her just a month prior to the trauma (we were celebrating my Holy Communion, and my sister's confirmation).

Dad suffered a broken shoulder bone and a broken leg, but the majority of his suffering was psychological. *Why did this happen to my wife? Why? Why? Why?*

In one sense my sister was lucky, as her only physical injury was a bruised eye when several pieces of glass penetrated through the skin of her forehead. But like all of us she suffered. "Why did mommy die?" she would ask the psychologist. How does anyone explain that to a child?

Jennifer De Pippo

Perhaps surprisingly, I didn't suffer as much psychologically as my dad and sister. I was too young to understand what had happened, and being asleep at the moment of the crash I didn't have to live with the terrifying memories of the event.

After 6 weeks of being in a coma, the neurologist responsible for me noted my progress. My eyes were open longer during therapy sessions and I would look at people when they spoke to me; but I still was non-responsive. I continued to make progress every day and eventually I was asked to shake my head to answer "no" and close my eyes to answer "yes". However, I still wasn't aware of my surroundings. It took several more weeks to regain my **consciousness**. I could not turn my head left because my right muscles were too weak. I didn't have any saliva control and the movements of my tongue were insufficient, making swallowing impossible. The nurses stimulated my mouth in

an unexpected MIRACLE

every which way to get me to eventually swallow. I was finally able to sit up straight so the nurses put me in a wheelchair.

As time progressed, I was able to control my neck movements. Since I couldn't communicate verbally, I was given a headpiece to point to pictures on the tray of my wheelchair to tell others what I needed. For example, if I was hungry, I would point to a picture of food; if I was tired, I would point to a picture of someone sleeping.

Looking back now, with that awful, frightening, and difficult time nearly twenty years behind me, I can see some of the positive effects it had on the rest of my life. Before the accident, I always used to take life for granted and would often do dangerous stunts. But now I know that life can end in a matter of seconds. What was supposed to be a relaxing day in the country turned to tragedy in the blink of an eye. Now, I live every moment and every day to the fullest; and I take advantage of every opportunity I get. I enjoy life as the gift that it is – because I know that it could end at any moment.

I remember several years ago I went camping in Fairmont, British Columbia with my step-nephew and -niece. They were still young, my step-nephew was seven and my step-niece was nine. I was talking with my step-nephew as to why I had a speech impairment (I don't think his parents ever made him aware of what happened). I told him that I was in a very bad car accident that almost killed me. That's when my nephew got curious:

"What do you mean you were almost killed?" he asked. "You were seven. How can someone die at seven? They have their whole life ahead of them."

I simply answered, "Life doesn't always work out the way you want it to; life is complicated; life is unfair. Life can hit you pretty hard and it's up to you to deal with the consequences. That's why it's important to live every day to the fullest, but to also be very aware of the potential consequences.

an unexpected MIRACLE

Always think about being safe; wearing a helmet when riding your bike or a seatbelt in the car might just save your life. I know it saved mine."

I could tell he was struggling to understand what I was saying. In his seven-year-old world he was indestructible – only old people died! But I knew that he trusted me, and I could see a glimmer of understanding as my words reshaped his view of the world.

Before my life took a wrong turn, I was a lot of things. I was smart, I was popular, I was the "teacher's pet," I played and goofed around, and I felt accepted by others. Everything I had been was shattered in a matter of seconds, like a terrorist attack on my body and mind. I had to rebuild my life from scratch.

It isn't possible to change what has happened in the past, but now I had the choice on how to write my future. No matter how hard life hit me I did everything in my power to turn my negative situation into a positive one. I chose the road of recovery. Nurses, doctors, and therapists helped me as much as they could, but the rest was up to me. How far could I push myself? That was the question that hung over me every single day for the next twenty years.

Chapter 2

Dad

In the immediate wake of the accident, I had a lot of people helping to keep me alive and to start me on the road to recovery. Each one of them performed their function well, appearing when they were needed and then disappearing when their role was complete. But through it all, from the moment I was wheeled out of the fourteen-hour surgery and for every day in the past twenty years, there has been one person who has been at my side. Without him, I would not be writing these words today.

My father has a typical Italian character – emotional, intense, full of passion. He has a deep accent in his voice that can make it hard to understand what he says. Instead of pronouncing the "th" sound he says the "d" sound. My father is a very caring but strict person. I am his angel. Every day since the accident he's had to deal with the consequences – and he's never shied away from his duty, from supporting me through the tough days in my recovery to guiding me through the turbulent transition years from adolescent to adult. He is my father, my mentor, and my coach.

"Come on Jennifer! I know you can do it!" Dad would always tell me. "If you try your hardest then you know you've done your best. And you're a fighter: if you think you can do better, then there's always a next time to prove it." These would be the encouraging words Dad would say to me no matter what I did.

For the duration of my recovery in the hospital, Dad was asked by the doctors to be there for me every step of the way. He came to the hospital every single day, whether I was still in my coma or not. He sat there day after day; sometimes he even stayed in my room overnight. He carried a lot of stress for me. Although he's never said it to me,

an unexpected MIRACLE

deep down in his heart I think he blames himself for my injury and it beats him up every day.

Dad never left my sight. He was there when I enrolled in physio, occupational, speech, and audio therapies at Marie Enfant (rehabilitation hospital). He was there through my times of embarrassment, sadness, and laughter. Sometimes the actions of a person are more powerful than their words.

Dad wanted to keep me happy. He wanted me to live like every other kid. He brought me to the movie theaters, he took me out to eat, and he let me play my favorite game of mini-putt. He was my teacher to the real world, to street life. Because of Dad I achieved my dreams, and with time, I was able to relearn a lot of things. Dad was my inspiration to stay determined and not give up.

Dad had my back. He was my protector; he never let me get into harm's way. He knew beyond my disability that I was a lovable, compassionate, determined human being. He never gave up on me.

Jennifer De Pippo

We fought my battle together, hand in hand. If I wasn't capable of doing something, Dad would step in and do it for me. But he knew that I had the potential and determination to get better, and he always encouraged instead of coddled. It is because of Dad that today I am a strong, independent woman.

Like me, Dad wasn't a quitter. He believed that I would recover because he knew that nothing is impossible. "Impossible" is not part of my dad's vocabulary. Anything is possible if you believe. Dad would always take care of me before he took care of himself. He always made sure that I had everything I needed. Nobody on the face of this earth can replace my dad.

Dad spoke straight with me. He told me what reality was like and prepared me to face it. "You have to be smart in life," he'd say to me. "Don't just trust everyone." Sometimes he would get mad at me but it was for my own good. Dad loves me no

an unexpected MIRACLE

matter what. He wants the best for me. He understands what I'm going through psychologically and he feels bad because he can't solve the problem. When Dad is around, I feel secure.

I am the product of my dad. He shaped me into what I am today. If he hadn't put me on the right path, encouraged me every step of the way, and continued to nurture my soul, I would have never reached the place I've reached today.

I remember clearly what Dad did for me. Whenever I had an "accident" in my pants, Dad would help me clean myself. Trust me, at 9 years old it was an embarrassment to need help from your father to clean yourself. When these accidents happened I wanted to disappear like a ghost. On more than one occasion I also wet the bed. I slept so deep that I couldn't tell my brain to wake me up to go to the bathroom. Once again, Dad would be there to help me change my bed. Dad was there for me after school when I came home feeling scared that something bad was going to happen to me. He'd talk to me, help me talk through it myself. Dad was there for me, protecting me when I stayed up long hours at night trying to get my homework done. Dad had a lot of patience with me.

In the best interests of my recovery, Dad separated me from my extended family. If I wasn't separated from them, my mind would have never developed because they wouldn't have helped me, they would have just treated me like that poor little kid that would never get better. *How can my own family think that?* Knowing this, Dad justified his reason to take me away from them until I reached adulthood.

While I was writing this book, Dad suffered a heart attack. Fortunately, his attack was caught at the same time he was having it, so he was fully conscious and able to communicate during his hospital stay before he went in for triple bypass

an unexpected MIRACLE

surgery. Sometimes I ask myself whether I was the cause of Dad's heart attack. I know that I didn't directly cause his heart failure, but I believe that I was a contributing factor. According to the doctors, stress was the major factor of the heart attack. Dad always stressed himself over me. He devoted himself entirely to helping me rehabilitate and become the woman I am today. He found a way to provide for me even during the difficult times.

What more can I say? I love my Dad.

Chapter 3

My road to recovery

It was a long road I began, those dim days in the summer of 1995, and at the time the future was far from certain. I'd already been on that road for a couple of months before I knew it myself, and it was September before I reconnected consciously.

All of a sudden, I opened my eyes and noticed that I was being rolled down the hallway of Sainte Justine Hospital and into an ambulance. I was now in a **vegetative state**.

"Where are they taking me?" was my first self-aware thought. At first I felt scared not knowing where I was going, but then I saw Dad was sitting right beside me and I knew that I was safe.

On September 7, 1995, I was transported by ambulance to Marie Enfant Hospital where I spent the next ten months in rehabilitation. This hospital had more of a homey feel. The unit was equipped

an unexpected MIRACLE

with a living room and kitchen. Food was far more appetizing than in a lot of other hospitals. More attention was given to preparing each meal because it was critical that the patients ate well to help them through their rehab.

It wasn't until sometime in late November of that year that I was fully aware of my surroundings. For those of you that have never experienced being in a coma (and I think that includes most of you) it takes time, sometimes too much, before the patient is in a conscious state. The therapies I needed to help me recover included physio, occupational, speech, audio, and special education. These therapies weren't easy – I had to focus 100% and have the determination to get better. I took each therapy every day, five times a week. I guess I could be compared to an Olympic athlete: an athlete has to focus on their sport, and they can't have any distractions. They have to train hard every day, and they need the drive and will to succeed.

Jennifer De Pippo

Until I was fully self-aware, I was fed formula through a feeding tube. It tasted awful on its way down to my stomach, but taking formula was the only option since I couldn't eat solids. All the nutrients I needed to rebuild myself came from the formula. When I'd fully regained consciousness I graduated to eating baby food. Good thing, too, because if I hadn't started eating baby food my feeding tube would have been moved from my nose to be inserted directly into my stomach, which would have left me with a scar there today.

I didn't have enough muscle control in my throat to help me swallow, but the nurses stimulated my throat muscles enough in four months that I was able to swallow pureed fruits and vegetables. This was my first time eating food that wasn't attached to a machine. The first bite of food I was ever fed felt and tasted so refreshing that my mouth just exploded with flavor.

an unexpected MIRACLE

When the time came to actually eat solids, I had to be very careful to chew properly and not choke. Eating became more of a chore of concentration than the pleasure of feeling satisfied. At first, I was fed by a nurse in the lunch room until I gained a proficient grasp of my fork and could lift my arm to my mouth. My movements weren't perfect but that was up to the therapy department to take care of. One food I couldn't eat for a while was peanuts. Allergies weren't a factor for me, but peanuts are not very kid-friendly. For beginners, they are very hard to chew and swallow without choking. Before I even attempted to eat peanuts or even certain chocolate bars, I had to learn to chew efficiently.

Because of the mass of feeding tubes and breathing hoses that crowded my throat, I developed swallowing disorders. Every time I had a bite to eat or a drink of water, strange gurgling and swallowing sounds would be audible to my audience. I had to force myself to swallow; nothing slid down on its own anymore.

Learning these basic functions of living again was hard enough, but they were just the beginning of my long road. My brain had to re-learn so many things like talking, walking and just the normal activities of life that I'd taken for granted before. Once I was fully self-aware and able to interact with other people more easily, I engaged in many kinds of therapy.

First of all, I had to take play therapy. Play therapy is the "kiddie" version of the process of working with a psychologist. During play therapy I usually did an activity, like drawing or coloring, and I would have to talk about what I did and how it made me feel. Usually the psychologist always found some sort of similarity between what I did and the accident I was in.

Physiotherapy has to deal with moving different body parts. It involves more stretching and muscle endurance techniques than aerobic exercises. My muscles had slowly deteriorated in the coma; physiotherapy brought the strength and endurance back. Physiotherapy often includes some form of swimming. It is easier for a patient to stand in water than on land because the buoyancy of the water supports their muscles. The buoyancy lifts the patient, making them feel lighter and making it easier for them to stand. Eventually, once their leg muscles build up, they can start to walk in the water. It's harder to move through water than on land because the water creates more resistance, but physiotherapists make their patients do the hard stuff first, knowing that the easy will just follow with time ... I like this philosophy.

Every day was a baby step towards overcoming the obstacles of relearning to walk. The drive within me helped me achieve my goal: I was determined to walk. In the beginning, like every patient, I did my physiotherapy in the pool. When I mastered exercises in the water, I started doing floor exercises to increase the strength and endurance in my legs. The next step was to learn to find my balance. I achieved this by gripping a bar on either side of my waist, just like the ones ballerinas use. Once I found my balance, I had to tell my brain to put one foot in front of the other. It was a slow and long process; it didn't come easy. Months went by until I was able to walk with a walker. Even more time went by before I could walk on my own.

Occupational therapy has to deal with, but is not limited to, motor skills. Being able to hold a pencil, buttoning buttons, circling letters, holding a fork, cutting with a knife, and balancing a glass of water are all examples of what this therapy consists of. The right side of my body was much weaker than my left, so in the beginning, I had to learn to be ambidextrous (I was right-handed). I had to learn to adapt. I performed a majority of the tasks I was asked to do with my left hand. Eventually, when I

an unexpected MIRACLE

started to regain my strength I started to make use of my right hand. But by then I didn't want to use my right because I'd become accustomed to using my left, and I found that I got better results if I used my left. But I knew I had to retrain my right, and I doggedly stuck with it. Occupational therapists work with patients to develop "self" skills needed to gain independence.

Speech therapy is all about learning to speak. Speech therapists make you work on exercising your vocal cords to project your voice. When I started speech therapy, I strained my vocal cords to speak, so my voice came out like a harsh, soft whisper. My therapist always told me to relax and let my voice come naturally ... not easy to do after spending six weeks in a coma. I tried to let my voice come naturally no matter how impossible it seemed because I knew nothing was impossible; I had the determination to speak again. In order to get me working on my voice, I was shown a series of pictures that I had to talk about. Pictures are truly worth a thousand words!

Audio therapy is designed to determine the level of your hearing – that is, how well your ears work. I was put into a sound-proof room with headphones on and the therapist talked to me from another sound-proof room (like a recording studio) through a microphone either into the right, left, or both ears. Sometimes I had to repeat what the therapist said to me. Sometimes she had me respond to beeping signals that were transmitted through my brain. And sometimes she spoke to me with her mouth covered, which was very revealing. The difficulty of understanding I had when I couldn't see her mouth told the therapist that I was relying on lip reading to understand people and therefore my hearing problems weren't being noticed so much. Audio therapy was performed every few weeks to see if there was any improvement with my hearing. Even today the nerve from my right ear to my brain is damaged; it has trouble sending quick messages so I can give a quick response. I am not totally deaf in my right ear; I can hear sounds but with a background of rushing sounds.

Another so-called therapy I took was special education. In this therapy I learned to socialize and play; to gain my independence. Coloring, painting, play-doh, building blocks, cut-and-paste, you name it. I did every constructive activity I could do. As part of special education, I made bi-weekly trips to my house with my educator in order to familiarize myself with its details. In the beginning my trips were a challenge because I was still in a wheelchair and had to be lifted up the stairs to get to the main floor (my house was a split-level).

This therapy taught me to gain my independence. Not only did the therapist make me do playful activities, but she engaged me in cooking classes with her. Once a week I made something in the kitchen. Learning the fundamentals of cooking and baking prepared me to take care of myself. I remember one week I made pasta for the entire unit; that was about thirty kids.

While I was in a coma I had to wear diapers. I still had to wear diapers immediately following my waking because I didn't know how to go to the bathroom. Something as easy as using the bathroom proved to be an obstacle. I felt the urge to go but, for some reason, my brain didn't connect the sensation to using the bathroom. It was extremely embarrassing when I had the occasional "accident" in my pants. When I was discharged from the hospital, I still had these accidents. I was so embarrassed when the accidents happened in public. I mean, come on, I was nine years old!

After several months of receiving intensive therapy, my progress was noted. Translated in English from French, the special education therapist wrote:

an unexpected MIRACLE

Jennifer moves independently without help. When walking on uneven surfaces, she must take extra precaution. She sometimes loses her balance when she gets tired. She is aware of her capabilities and controls herself well.

When several kids in the unit go swimming on Monday nights, Jennifer does not use floaters. She needs supervision in the pool because she over-estimates her capabilities and endurance in the deep end (five feet deep).

Jennifer is independent in her everyday activities. She only needs supervision like the other kids her age.

*Jennifer has a hearing **impairment** in her right ear. To adapt, Jennifer places herself next to the person who is talking to her and she faces them. She understands others by reading their lips. It is important that Jennifer is able to hear especially when there is a lot of noise around. Jennifer makes me repeat myself regularly.*

Jennifer talks and expresses her needs. There isn't a lot of variation in the pitch of her voice and she is missing the control of the loudness of her voice. When she is in a group or a loud environment she has to pay attention extra hard.

*Jennifer doesn't demonstrate facial expressions (**impairment** of facial features) but should get better with time. She knows she doesn't demonstrate these expressions but "corrects" herself when asked by an adult.*

Jennifer is well oriented in time and space. She has taken charge of the time and is never late for her therapies.

Jennifer organizes herself by herself. When finished an activity, Jennifer cleans her mess and puts her tools away. She needs explanation when doing a new activity so she can organize herself well. Jennifer has a good memory.

Jennifer has gotten into the habit of doing homework. She is starting to organize herself more and more. Jennifer is capable of concentrating her attention on a subject.

an unexpected MIRACLE

Jennifer is more and more aware of her limits but she doesn't always like the results she gets.

She reacts impulsively to other kids. She doesn't know how to react sociably. Therefore, Jennifer pulls herself out of the group. Jennifer occasionally needs help adequately expressing her emotions.

Jennifer will be discharged from the hospital on June 21, 1996. Jennifer will enroll in a day camp for her needs.

Because I was enrolled in school before the accident, I needed to relearn the academics so a teacher came to the hospital twice a week to teach me third grade material (I would have been going into grade three in September of '96). This was a challenge for me because while I had to keep the will and determination in the therapies I took, I also had to motivate myself to relearn school material. My teacher tracked my progress. Here is a report she wrote to present at a conference:

Jennifer De Pippo

Although Jennifer will tell you that she does not like to read, she is quite successful in Language Arts. On the SORT Oral Reading Test, which evaluates word recognition, she placed at the 3.3 grade level. In reading Comprehension she is in the high grade two range. She prefers Spelling and tasks with specific responses, for example puzzles that require filling in missing letters or matching items... She relishes the sense of success that comes with more precise work that yields clear-cut solutions...

In Mathematics she recalled quite clearly the experience of having learned certain concepts in school in grade two. She was familiar with a variety of skills she had previously learned but occasionally will confuse addition with subtraction if there is a change from one operation to another unexpectedly. With cues and reminders when she is working, she is very adept at coming up with correct solutions. Jennifer has begun learning the two's, three's, and five's times tables. This is

an unexpected MIRACLE

new information for her. She has a good understanding of new concepts and remembers what she has learned.

At present, Jennifer is able to concentrate for periods from 30-40 minutes. She takes school seriously and is able to keep her materials well organized. In fact, she becomes quite impatient with anyone that doesn't do the same. Change seems to be difficult for her to deal with and if there is a variation in schedule it is important to explain to her why there has been a change and what it will mean for her. Once things are clear, she is quite cooperative. Jennifer's strong personality and determination is a positive driving force that motivates her toward continued progress in her school work.

Three months after I was hospitalized, the nurses finally told me that my mom had died in the car accident. I didn't take it very well and started a tantrum. I got so aggressive that the nurses had to strap me down to my bed until I calmed down. It wasn't a pretty picture.

Jennifer De Pippo

For the Christmas holiday season, Dad hung Christmas lights around the ceiling of my room (I was in a private room for the first several months). I loved looking up at the ceiling at night with lights of red, green, and blue shining down on me. It really dressed up the bare walls of my room: the lights made me feel happy! I think Dad was trying to make me remember Christmas and what it looked like. I felt pretty special. I was the only one that had Christmas lights hung in their room.

You can recover from a brain injury no matter how old you are. The process for my brain to reconnect and rewire itself was easy because I was still a child and my brain was still developing. However, it is possible for an older person to recover as well. All that is needed is a little determination. Our brains are always plastic; they are malleable; they are **neuroplastic**. The brain is very complex, but its fundamental power operates under this mantra: use it or lose it. Our brain is

an unexpected MIRACLE

made up of different "brain maps," each of which corresponds to a different activity we normally do. Without exercising our brain maps, we will eventually lose them. The lost brain map will be repurposed to help another area of the brain.

For example, we all have a brain map for computing numbers, but if we always let our calculator compute answers for us, our brain map will lose the ability to process numbers and an adjacent map, such as music, will expand and take over the map for computing numbers. Some brain exercises you can do on a budget include: washing dishes (doing a circular motion), reading (word recognition), doing Sudoku (challenging the mind to sequence numbers), and cooking (concentrating on cutting food with a knife and making sure not to burn the food). If money isn't an issue you might consider joining your local gym. It benefits your mind as well as your body.

Jennifer De Pippo

Many people came to visit me in the hospital. Dad came every day, but so did many other people. My aunt, uncle, and grandparents from my mother's side visited me almost every night, and they usually brought gifts for me. I remember that they brought me a chocolate egg for Easter, my aunt bought me the movie *Miracle on 34th Street* for Christmas (I love that movie!), and my grandmother made me egg pasta (but I couldn't eat it, the nurses wouldn't allow it) when I started eating solids. My grandmother's brother came to visit me with his wife. My former neighbors and best friend stopped by when I least expected. My second grade homeroom teacher, Madame Natalie, surprised me when I had my afternoon "siesta" for relaxation. After all, Italians stick together!

After I was discharged from the hospital on June 21, 1996, a **neuropsychologist** followed up with me at the end of August. He conducted an exam on me

an unexpected MIRACLE

to see the progress of my brain. The following are his conclusions:

The trauma Jennifer suffered had some major consequences on her cognitive functions. It is difficult for her to involve herself in what she is doing. She has certain difficulties with her lexical access, an occasional appeal to the salient stimulus, attentional difficulties in terms of working memory and cleverness to juggle multiple ideas at once. She has both a verbal and visuospatial disability. She was not only slower in her motor skills, but also the level of mental flexibility in passing from one concept to the next.

In return, Jennifer could learn both visually and visuospatially if taught correctly. She was able to perform verbal memorization. She has good resistance for interference and can keep information stored in her memory.

When Jennifer is at school she has to take into account her fatigue. She has to foster an adequate

Jennifer De Pippo

environment that allows her to adequately organize her information. Despite her successes, Jennifer has trouble multi-tasking.

In September of 1996, I enrolled in Mackay Center; a rehabilitation school. A lot of hearing impaired and deaf students attended (I had to learn the basics of American Sign Language), but also the students who needed to take therapy. The school program was more about adapting to the "real" world than about learning the academics. The teaching was really slow because students often left the classroom to take therapy. Once a week my class participated in swimming lessons, and once a month (ten times out of the year) we went on a field trip. In terms of the academics, Mackay Center was a walk in the park. But on the other hand, I had to maintain my focus on my therapies and I couldn't spend countless hours on my school work. At Mackay Center, and every year after that, I had an

an unexpected MIRACLE

Individual Program Plan (IPP). An IPP usually states the modifications that need to be done in the classroom to meet my needs, but since Mackay Centre specialized in meeting my needs, my IPP dealt more with the areas where I needed improvement:

Education Status:

Jennifer is following a regular grade three program. She has difficulty with fine motor skills such as printing, writing and art.

Jennifer is reading at grade level with excellent comprehension. She enjoys sharing her books to the class.

Jennifer can write a short story with a good beginning and ending. She would rather print than use the computer because she wants to increase her speed (now I would rather use the computer).

In mathematics, Jennifer is successfully following Challenging Math grade 3.

Jennifer is responsible for her work.

Jennifer De Pippo

Hearing Status:

Jennifer used an FM system in the classroom and is being followed by audiology. Jennifer has a moderate loss in her right ear.

Visual Status:

Dad reports that Jennifer's eyesight has been checked and that it is fine.

Medical Status:

*Jennifer is followed every six months by **Neurology** at Sainte Justine's Hospital. Her next appointment is next July. Jennifer is a healthy student that is rarely seen in the Medical department.*

Communication Status: (speech/language communication status)

Jennifer communicates verbally and is able to make herself understood in most situations. Jennifer can have

an unexpected MIRACLE

*difficulty understanding what is said to her, due to a hearing loss and to auditory processing problems. Jennifer has a slow rate of speech and a somewhat flat effect (probably due to a moderate **dysarthria**). She has a somewhat strained vocal quality.*

Psychosocial Status:

Cognitive:

- Displays good attention and concentration
- Displays appropriate problem-solving strategies
- **Visual-perceptual** skills are age appropriate
- Independently organizes herself for an activity, including materials and sequencing the steps to complete the task

Behaviour:

Jennifer De Pippo

- Very determined; displays good perseverance during more challenging activities

Mobility Status (Ongoing):

- Walks independently, can fall if running quickly
- Slightly unsteady on stairs, therefore a question of safety, if no railing going down. Comfortable with no railing going up.
- Negotiates all surfaces and inclines. Steps do lack grading so is at risk of easier than normal mishaps.

Fine Motor Status:

- Right hand dominant, but uses left hand for some activities (eg. Manipulating small objects) due to better control (less **ataxia**) on left.

an unexpected MIRACLE

- Mature pencil grasp but difficulty with pencil control (quality and speed) due to **ataxia**; quality of pencil skills has improved since September 1996.

- Tremor influences the accuracy, quality and speed of performance on fine motor skills (right hand affected more than left hand)

- Very slow speed of performance eg writing, cutting

- Areas of weakness: upper-limb coordination, speed and **dexterity**, and **visual-motor** control.

Self Help Status:

- Independent eating, grooming/hygiene, toileting and dressing (difficulty fastening small buttons only).

Short Term Plan and Activities:

Jennifer De Pippo

Education:

- Jennifer needs to have friends.

Occupational Therapy: (ongoing)

- To improve upper limb coordination, including **bilateral coordination**.
- To improve upper limb speed and **dexterity**
- To improve **visual-motor** control skills.

Jennifer will:

- Fasten small buttons (1/4") on a garment independently.
- Complete classroom writing assignments with greater speed.
- Display an improved score on the Beery Development Test of Visual-Motor Integration.

an unexpected MIRACLE

Physiotherapy: (ongoing)

- Needs to increase range in tight hamstrings and increase strength in certain muscle groups in her legs such as the hip abductors, knee extensors, and plantar flexors.
- Difficulties with smoothness of movement, **grading** of movement, and **coordinated** movement in physical performance especially as physical activities become more complicated. Experiences more difficulty with the right side of her body.
- Difficulties with challenging gross motor performance ie heel walking, single limb stance, hopping, skipping, ball activities, bicycle riding
- **Kyphosis** posture – tends to keep her head and eyes down as she walks.

Jennifer De Pippo

- Needs to improve her level of fitness – aerobically and strength-wise.

Jennifer will:

- Do stretching exercises for her hamstrings, and strengthening exercises for her hip abductors, quadriceps, and plantar flexors during therapy at school with a home program at home.
- Practice gross motor activities aimed at improving smoothness, **grading**, and **coordination**.
- Work on challenging gross motor activities to improve balance and stability. Such activities include standing on one leg, toe stance on one leg, hopping, skipping, running backwards, ball skills, bicycling.
- Strengthen antigravity postural muscles and work on using a better posture during walking and sitting.

- Participate in a "step-class" to improve general aerobic fitness and will do general strengthening exercises ie abdominals, push-ups.

Communication:

- Jennifer needs to learn strategies to compensate for her hearing loss and processing difficulties.
- She needs to follow the **rules of pragmatics**.
- She needs to learn problem solving strategies
- She needs to improve her vocal quality and minimize the effects of the **dysarthria**.

Jennifer will:

- Learn strategies to help compensate for her hearing and processing difficulties.

Jennifer De Pippo

- Work on the **rules of pragmatics** (will follow an in-class program devised by the teacher, psychologist, and the speech therapist)
- Learn problem-solving strategies.
- Be given a home program of daily exercises for voice quality and facial muscle tone.

During my year at Mackay Centre, I proved to the teacher that I was too smart for the slow pace of learning, and I was transferred to the full academic school of St. Ignatius, where I was placed in fourth grade. Leaving a school that accepted me the way I was to attend another school where I didn't fit in was very hard on me. But, that was one of the challenges I had to face. The students isolated me from their groups. I'll never know exactly why but I think they never talked to me because I demonstrated negative body language. Maybe the

an unexpected MIRACLE

reason was just jealousy; jealousy that I performed better than the other students when I was considered "handicapped." Either way, I had to accept the fact other kids looked at me as being "different."

Chapter 4

My wish is granted...

When I was eleven years old, two years after my discharge from the hospital, a lady came to our house and told me she was my fairy godmother. This lady was from the Make-a-Wish Foundation of Quebec. She said that she was sent to me to grant me one wish (all the expenses would be paid by the Foundation) because she knew the tough times I was going through, dealing with a life-threatening illness (not fatal but one that won't go away). She would like me to forget about my obstacles for just one day by letting her create my one and only fantasy dream.

"Honey, what is the one thing you would wish for?" she asked.

"Gee, I don't know," I answered.

"Some people wish to meet celebrities, some wish to travel, some wish to go on an adventure...

an unexpected MIRACLE

the list goes on and on. I'll give you an example. Two of the wishes I granted were for cancer patients.

"One wish was for a girl who hated going shopping with everyone staring at her bald head. She didn't have a dad anymore and her mom couldn't afford to buy her a wig. Her wish was to go shopping with nobody around; just her, her mom, and some employees. So, we closed down the mall to the public for an entire morning and opened just for her. We took the wish one step further and we bought her a new wig," she explained.

"The second wish I granted was for a little boy suffering from leukemia. He loved going on rides, so he wished to go to Disneyworld. He got a VIP pass that enabled him to skip the long line-ups and go right to the front of the line to go on a ride. He spent three days on the grounds and then I sent him and his family off on a cruise with Disney. He had a blast. If you can dream it in your wildest dreams, I can make it become a reality."

This lady's response made me excited, but, at the same time, I felt overwhelmed. My mind went into overload thinking of all the places I wanted to go and all the people I wanted to meet. What would make me the happiest? I had to choose carefully.

"So I can wish for absolutely anything in the world?" I asked, still in disbelief.

"If you can think of it and see it, I will do everything possible to make your wish become a reality. You don't have to give me an answer today. Take your time to think about it. Make sure your wish comes from your heart. I'm going to have to ask you for your top three wishes; I won't grant you all three, but in case I can't grant you your first wish I will move on to your second and/or third. When you have your wishes all thought out, your dad can always contact me by phone. This is for you. I want to make you shine. In order for me to grant you

an unexpected MIRACLE

your wish your dad has to find another adult to come with you because if your sister wants to go somewhere and you want to go somewhere else you need two adults."

So that night I thought about it long and hard. I thought and thought and thought. Then it clicked! I loved eating ice cream, loved to swim, and I enjoyed sun tanning, so logically I would wish to go somewhere warm next to the water ...but where? Then my dad suggested that I wish to go on a cruise.

"Yes," I said, "that's it! For my first wish, I wish to go on a Caribbean cruise. If I can't go on a Caribbean cruise then I wish to go on a Mediterranean cruise. If I can't go on a Mediterranean cruise, I wish to go on a Trans-Atlantic cruise."

Dad contacted my fairy godmother and told her my three wishes. We anxiously waited at home for a phone call back. Around two weeks had gone by without hearing whether I would get my first wish or not. Then one afternoon, after I got home from school, the phone rang. My dad answered it and greeted my fairy godmother. She said that she was going to grant my first wish ... to go on a Caribbean cruise.

When I found out I jumped up and down with joy. "Yeah! I'm going on a cruise! All right!"

The only trouble for me was that the cruise was in April, over spring break, and it was now only January. I had to wait two long months before I got my wish! I started counting down the days.

I remember the night before we were to catch our flight to Florida: I couldn't sleep. I guess the excitement of knowing that I was going somewhere that I wanted to go made me more anxious than tired. I even caught a little cold that night. I just couldn't wait to board. In bed I thought of all the things I wanted to do on the ship. The more I

an unexpected MIRACLE

thought, the more excited I got. It seemed like time was running too slow and tomorrow would never come.

Soon enough I was off to Florida. We landed the night before our departure and got to stay in a hotel for the night. My sister and I stayed in one hotel room, and my dad and step-mom (Dad had re-married) stayed in another. Boy, was I ever comfortable; I had a whole queen size bed all to myself! The next morning we took a shuttle to the ship. All we had to do was get onto the ship – our luggage would be taken care of by the employees. At the ship, we were greeted by Captain Daffy Duck, who welcomed us aboard the *Big Red Boat*; a 3-day, 4-night Looney Tunes Cruise. It was a rather small ship; only 700 passengers. We sailed to Nassau, Bahamas, a beautiful but small island. We received state-of-the-art first class service. All my family was catered to. The Make-a-Wish Foundation worked their magic and made my family and I shine.

I hardly got any sleep, that first night in my cabin, thinking excitedly of all the things I wanted to do. And the next morning I decided to tackle first things first: I wanted to eat. Most of all, I wanted to eat all the ice cream I possibly could. I devoured bowls of ice cream like I was someone who never ate. The food in the dining room was exquisite; the food was prepared to perfection and every plate was like a painting, carefully arranged to perfection. Maybe my eyes were hungrier than my stomach, or the change of atmosphere made me that much hungrier, but I couldn't stop eating. The food looked too appetizing. During the day, I enjoyed sitting on the deck sun tanning by the pool. The hot rays of the sun were calming. I fell asleep under the sun. I protected my skin with sunscreen, but I still got a sunburn. Thankfully my sun burn wasn't too

an unexpected MIRACLE

severe. I cooled down in the pool when my skin got too warm.

On the second night of the cruise, I got tucked into bed by the Tasmanian Devil. He gave me a souvenir of a Looney Tunes pillow case and a miniature stuffed animal of himself. I took a picture with him before I hit the sack. I must have misplaced that picture because I can't find it anywhere! But all that matters is the memory I have of that night.

The time on board passed by fast: it seemed as if we disembarked the day after we arrived. But I left the cruise ship feeling energized and full of life. While the cruise may have been just a few days, it created a lifetime of great memories, but even more than that it gave me something that until then I had been lacking.

It gave me the hope that I had lost. The hope that I could have a better future. Today I am living that hope and I am creating that better future for myself.

Chapter 5

Am I afraid, or are they?

Three years after the accident, Dad decided to move us to western Canada. On June 29, 1998 my dad, step-mom, sister and I loaded up the car for the three-day drive from Montreal to Calgary. We came to Alberta in the hopes of a new beginning and a better future.

One of the advantages of coming to the West was that I didn't have to speak French anymore; sometimes speaking French proved to be a challenge for me on its own. In Alberta I started performing better in school for two reasons: one, I didn't have to translate everything I learned from French to English and vice versa, and two, my teachers were much more patient with me. Back in 1998, Calgary was a much smaller city, probably one-fifth the size of Montreal with a population of

Jennifer De Pippo

200,000 people. Grown-ups in Calgary seemed nicer and much more polite.

The year we moved to Calgary I went into Grade 5 at St. Dominic Elementary School. I dealt with a lot of emotional bullying; much of the same stuff I dealt with in Montreal. The majority of the kids isolated me from their groups when they formed teams to play tag or soccer because I was too slow to keep up. Kids always wanted to run, run, run. I was always the last one chosen for a group project when we (the students) got to choose our own groups, and I always ended up doing most of the work. Over the years, I had no choice but to grow accustomed to solitude.

The kids didn't understand that I had auditory processing problems; they just made fun of me. I will never forget the prank they liked playing on me:

"Jennifer, what's the first letter of the alphabet?" they asked.

an unexpected MIRACLE

"Eh?" I responded.

"Jennifer, what's the first letter of the alphabet?" they asked again.

"A", I responded.

And like so it would continue...

Kids can be terrible bullies. I wonder now if their aggression was driven out of fear. I was different, and some people are afraid of anything that's different.

Thankfully I only had to put up with the immaturity of these kids for two years. After that I was off to St. Jean Brebeuf Junior High. I spent the next three years in this school for Grades 7, 8, and 9. Things started to calm down; even though I was still isolated, kids left me alone and didn't cause trouble. Because I didn't have any friends or a social life, I devoted all of my time to my school work. I started doing exceptionally well in school again and I proved to everyone that I was smart regardless of my disability. My motivator was to set my goals high. I worked longer hours than many other students, but my hard work paid off.

I received numerous awards. I was awarded Excellence every year in junior high for maintaining a general average of at least 85%, and in Grade 8 I received a certificate for maintaining the highest mark throughout the year in French (ironically enough!) and Religion. One award I received really stood out: The St. Jean Brebeuf Award, in recognition of my commitment and dedication to the school community.

For the three years of senior high, I went to St. Francis High School. In high school I assumed that students would be more mature, but that wasn't the case. There were always two types of people: the mature, like those on Student Council who were thoughtful and patient, and the immature—the ones that didn't care about others. I had a tough time in high school because I felt overwhelmed by the fast pace of learning, but I started to get involved with

an unexpected MIRACLE

the mature kids and joined Student Council. I managed to find the determination within me to push myself to new limits and I graduated within the three-year time frame. Students with disabilities often take longer to graduate because they can't manage a full course load. I graduated in a class of 657 students; the largest graduating class in the history of the school.

Because I didn't have any friends in junior high, I'd decided to stay home for my ninth grade graduation party. The year I graduated from senior high I competed against several other honor students to be the graduating class valedictorian. I didn't win that honour, but I did win the opportunity to give a toast to the graduates at the banquet. At that moment I felt special; all the hard work I'd put into the competition paid off.

When my dad found out what I'd won, he grew furious and overprotective.

"Do you think people will want to listen to you after they drank all day?" he demanded. "You with your flat voice? And remember the food that was served at your sister's graduation banquet? It was disgusting!" Eventually he calmed down and told me his real concerns. "Please Jen, don't go, for your own sake. I don't want people to laugh at you and make you feel embarrassed."

He was afraid for me, but not without justification. Through high school I'd dealt with the isolation that comes from being avoided and, possibly, feared, for being different. It was sad that all of us were caught up in our own fears, but I trusted my dad's wisdom and declined to give the toast.

Instead I ended up going out with my family to a fancy Italian restaurant called *Da Guido*. The food was delicious. And looking back now I don't think I missed much the night of the banquet. I wouldn't have had anybody to socialize with, and I heard

an unexpected MIRACLE

stories at school the next day that the food was awful. I did regret not being able to give a speech, but my dad was probably right and it would've been embarrassing for me.

To be honest, I was used to missing out on things. Over the years I missed out on much more than just graduations. After the accident I missed out on the remaining ten years of my childhood. Lying in the hospital I had to grow up fast. My injuries forced me to relearn the basics of living, which left little or no time to just live like a kid. I missed out on playing with my friends in my neighborhood; I missed out on participating in extra-curricular activities; I missed out on getting invited to birthday parties; and I missed out on the overall feeling of being a kid. I think I speak for every person recovering from an injury as well as for myself: when a traumatic incident happens in your life, you mature much faster. You mature in the sense of taking life seriously, not as a big joke like when you were a kid. You are more cautious about your surroundings, and you would rather not do dangerous things like you did before your tragedy.

After high school, I went on to college and took an accounting diploma. As always, I pushed my limits, and until then I'd never known how far I could go because I'd never reached too far. But at college I started to hit those limits academically. I really struggled with the concepts they were teaching, and eventually I realized that I might not succeed in a place where I'd always done so well—school! I started to feel depressed all the time; I was always in the counselor's office. To add to the pressure, I knew that college was pretty pricey, and I wanted to make sure the money my dad paid for me to go to school wasn't wasted. Ultimately it just became too much. I was scared… plain scared. I ultimately wasn't able to complete the diploma, but to me all that matters is that I'd had the drive to try

an unexpected MIRACLE

to push all the way my limits, the limits most people don't even attempt to reach.

In the summer of 2009, I moved with my dad and step-mom to Cranbrook, British Columbia. This was the best move yet. Just like moving to Calgary had been a new beginning for me, moving to Cranbrook was an even better and newer beginning. Cranbrook is a much smaller city (there are only 20 000 people) and it's easy for me to get around on foot. I love walking the same way many people do – it's relaxing and refreshing – but I'd say I love it even more than most. It's amazing how much you can appreciate something that you lost and then worked for years to regain.

Looking back on my years in Calgary, I'd hoped they would be a new beginning for me. In some ways they were but in other ways not. It was a new beginning in terms of leaving my past behind, but the emotional bullying that I endured was no different. Just like in Montreal, most of the Calgary kids were mean. They thought I didn't deserve to enroll in a regular program, let alone excel at it. In their opinion, I was "handicapped."

But what does that really mean? The truth is, almost everyone is handicapped or has some sort of disability; we just might not consider it a disability because the defect is common in a lot of people. For example, wearing braces is a disability because your teeth have gone crooked. Wearing glasses means you have a vision disability, walking with a cane, walker, or crutches because you broke a limb or suffer from arthritis means you have a disability with your bones. Being an alcoholic or a smoker is a disability because both are addictive and they both damage your brain.

I have a brain injury but I'm not stupid. When most people meet me, they jump to a conclusion too quickly and assume that I'm stupid. They don't give me a chance to prove them wrong. The damaged functions in the right hemisphere of my brain limit

an unexpected MIRACLE

my non-verbal communication, but the rest of my brain functions just like anybody else's. The brain is complex. The process of writing or painting derives from the right hemisphere but works in correlation with the left hemisphere to carry out the task. I'm a bit slower at doing things because of the disconnect between my brain's two hemispheres, but that hardly makes me stupid.

We live in a discriminative society. From experience I've learned that people tend to isolate the people that appear to be in the minority. Society assumes that because someone is different they are not approachable. I've lived through enough of those days. I've decided to find the courage within me to stand up for myself. If others give me a chance, they will realize that I am just like them.

I'm not happy to just hide on the fringes and let people assume that I'm stupid, or different, or in some way "unapproachable." I realize that other people aren't going to make the first move, so if I want to make an impression I have to make the first move.

I was at my gym recently, and I'd noticed that there was a man who was often there at the same time of day as me. I'd do my workout and he'd do his, but even though we spent so much time in such close proximity I never saw a friendly glance or gesture from him toward me. So I decided to approach him: "Are you afraid of me?"

"No," he answered, clearly startled at my blunt question. "Why would you think that?"

"Because you never talk to me. We're both here nearly every day and I feel like you're ignoring me. If so, I'll go away."

"No," he said, meeting my eyes and smiling genuinely. "I'm just concentrating on my routine. I don't mind talking to you."

I explained right away that my odd-sounding speech was due to a brain injury from many years ago, but that I was a normal person.

an unexpected MIRACLE

"To me you're just like anybody else," he said. "If you hadn't told me, I wouldn't have known you'd suffered from a brain injury. I don't think there's anything wrong with you."

His name, if you haven't guessed, is Bill Roberts, the loveable old miner who wrote the foreword to this book.

From that day we became good friends. It was actually a good lesson for me. I realized that I'd become so used to being shunned that my default assumption toward anyone who didn't talk to me was that they were afraid of me. It's certainly true that a lot of people are afraid of me, and every other "different" person, and I still think this is unjust. But it's up to me to take the initiative, speak up for myself and tell others that I am just like them. And sometimes I get a pleasant surprise, like when I meet a nice person like my friend Bill from the gym.

In Cranbrook, I've been able to take control of my independence. I've found a place to belong; I've found the Fitness Incorporated gym and I go there six times a week, no excuses. I do all kinds of cardio and weight-lifting exercises: leg extensions, squats, back, core, biceps, triceps, and balance. It helps me maintain my physical fitness as well as my strength and endurance like the couple of years I spent in physiotherapy. The cardio I do helps my balance and to maintain momentum. One exercise that really helps is the speed cycling class. In this class I cycle on a stationary bike with different resistances on the pedals. The best part is I don't have to worry not being properly coordinated or falling off the bike and making a fool of myself. I enjoy the class; it's a lot of fun. Ever since I joined in October 2012, I've noticed more definition in my arms, legs and shoulders. There are many benefits physically and health-wise to getting involved with a gym, but going to the gym is also a social place; a place where I can meet new people and gain my confidence.

Chapter 6

Living with my own fears

There are many obstacles I face every day. Ever since I turned 13 and started venturing out on my own, I started suffering from anxiety and depression. Just like there is a good and bad side to everything, there is a good and bad side of anxiety.

Good anxiety is beneficial to me because it gives me a boost in my endorphins—"feel-good" hormones. Good anxiety plays its role when I get excited, connect with others socially, or when I want to achieve the best results.

Most of the time, though, I experience bad anxiety.

My mind creates phantasms and illusions of me harming myself with my surroundings. Because of this, I'm scared of just about everything around me. I experience anxiety by simply walking down the street. When I walk on the sidewalk and see cars coming towards me, I get anxious that I am going to jump in front of a car. Or when I walk by a pile of big rocks on the ground, I get anxious because I think that I will take a rock and bang it on my head. When I walk past a sewer, I get anxious and think that I am going to drop my personal belongings down the holes and lose them forever. Or when I get into the vehicle to go somewhere, I get anxious when the speed accelerates because I think that I will jump out and kill myself. When a campfire is lit, I think that I will jump into the fire. Similarly, when a burner is on, I panic that I will burn myself or set the house on fire. Knives are used to cut food, right? Well, my anxiety makes me think that I will kill myself; that I will stick a knife in my throat. I can't walk up a mountain or stay in a room in a high-rise with a balcony because I get these images in my head that I will jump and kill myself.

These thoughts are all very disturbing. Even though I am smart enough to know not to do certain

an unexpected MIRACLE

things, I still panic because I feel and envision that I am going to do it. This is when my anxiety reaches its peak; I start to perspire, my heart rate increases, and I start to feel hungry. My anxiety becomes a panic attack.

Some of the anxieties I have are flashbacks. When my mind sees a dangerous incident on television or in real life, the scene gets stored in the back of my mind, so when a similar situation arises in my own life, my mind reminds me of the incident and tells me to worry that the outcome will not be pleasant. My mind tells me to be extra cautious. My mind is constantly thinking of the dangers I can encounter. The flashbacks I experience seem so real that they wake me up at night and make me want to yell at the top of my lungs. I got a second chance in life and I don't want to waste it by doing something stupid.

Back in Grade 7 we watched the movie *Lord of the Flies* as part of our social studies class. The anxiety and the fear I experience toward rocks has ties to this movie. There were two groups of kids fooling around (or something) on a mountain. One group was up higher than the other, so the higher group threw a rock down a cliff onto one of the head of a kid from the other group. The kid from the other group was killed instantly. I didn't know the situation but I clearly remember the scene. This is why I get anxious when I see a rock. My mind turns what it sees into reality.

For example, my dad, step-mom and I camped in Fairmont, BC the summer before we moved to Cranbrook. Everything was going fine until the next morning when we drove from the campsite back to town. We were on the highway and I remember experiencing the sensation of wanting to jump out of the vehicle. For some reason, I felt the car accelerating to far too high of a speed. I began to feel unsteady. To add to the problem, the doors on the vehicle didn't lock automatically, so I thought I

an unexpected MIRACLE

was going to open the door and jump out. I was so scared. I tried to control my temptation. I grasped the hand-hold in front of me and prayed that I would be all right. From that day on I avoided going anywhere near a highway in a car with doors that don't lock automatically.

Another event that triggered my anxiety was when I went on a hike with a friend in Fairmont, BC. I didn't expect just a simple hike to make me dwell on the event afterwards. My friend and I walked through a rocky path up a hill. We walked pretty far when all of a sudden we came across a waterfall with a strong current. We stood over a shrine of the lifeguard that drowned trying to cross to get to the other side of the river. At that moment it was interesting to see, but that night I started having flashbacks that I would go in the water and drown too. It was scary.

One day we walked up the Hoodoo Mountains in Fairmont, BC. I was calm until we got to the top to look at the country down below. I started to panic—there wasn't anything to keep visitors from jumping off the side of the mountain. I visualized myself jumping off the cliff; it wasn't a pretty scene. I did not want to sightsee on the mountain anymore. I wanted to get off the mountain. I was so scared, I felt like crying; I wanted to go back to the campsite.

I experienced another episode of a flashback when I went to Las Vegas with my dad and stepmom. We stayed on the Las Vegas Strip: the best place, apparently, to have a series of flashbacks. People who've had too much to drink, people asking for charity (specifically beer), homeless people, and most importantly, high-rises with balconies occupying every single space on the strip. I couldn't fall asleep at night because I was petrified…petrified because I slept in a room by myself on the twelfth floor. Visions in my head made me believe that I was going to jump over the balcony and kill myself. I was so scared. I wanted to yell as loud as I could until someone came to check on me. My anxiety skyrocketed. I felt like crying. I was so scared that the night seemed to last forever; the clock was ticking but the hands on the clock didn't move.

Because of my experiences with anxiety, I try to stay calm and not get too emotional. However, when I get mad, my anxiety reaches levels of extremity and I start to feel sick; my heart rate speeds up, my blood pressure sky-rockets and I start to perspire like a pig. This, as you might imagine, isn't pleasant to experience so I take every precaution not to reach this level. I've looked into taking anti-depressant and/or anxiety pills, but my problem isn't the kind of depression or anxiety that those pills are designed to counter: the problem is that my brain suffered a massive trauma and is still injured. It's not even like I have a brain condition like bipolar disorder or schizophrenia – my case is unique to my circumstances.

I experience situations of depression when I think of the things I would like to have. For instance, I would like to have close friends; I would like to date; I would like it if people treated me with more respect (something I don't get a lot of).

A lot of people recommend yoga to reduce anxiety, but I think the meditation aspect is what helps the most. Meditation is basically about concentration – concentration on whatever I am doing. When I eat, I meditate because I am concentrating on the flavors and textures in my mouth. Now that I am writing my life story I have to concentrate on thinking of words and how they fit together in a sentence.

Anxiety creeps up on me like a ghost, triggered deep in my mind; I never know when I'll experience it. Funny enough, possibly the best solution when my anxiety is triggered in a matter of seconds is to

an unexpected MIRACLE

snack. I am constantly hungry when I experience anxiety; I have an appetite like a horse. I find that my brain needs food to help me calm down and get my mind to concentrate on something else. In this regard, my body needs the energy and extra calories to fight off "the enemy," the anxiety. Our brain is like our stomach; they need to feel satisfied. Food is fuel for the brain.

I find that if I deprive myself of food, I immediately start to feel depressed. Carbohydrates, especially sweets, make my brain calm down. Our brains run on sugar. Pasta is known for its antidepressant qualities, so it is beneficial for me to eat pasta when I feel depressed (I like my pasta firm to the bite; in Italian we call that "al dente"). An alternative to eating is to chew gum. Gum works just as well because it releases a flavor into my mouth and triggers my brain to calm down just like food.

Jennifer De Pippo

As you can imagine, using food as a cure for anxiety could lead to other health problems, but fortunately I've discovered another excellent way to deal with my anxiety: exercise. When I'm exercising, my anxiety reduces to such a low state that it seems to be non-existent. However, as soon as I finish my exercise routine, my anxiety is retriggered.

I experience severe panic attacks when I'm alone. I feel overwhelmed. I think everything in my environment is a threat. I can't concentrate ... I just worry, worry that something will happen to me. To help alleviate my symptoms, I try to avoid watching scary and violent movies. Sometimes I can't even watch TV because my mind creates images even when I'm watching a family show. My mind usually starts to think negatively when I am not doing something constructive. When I don't have any other option but to stay home alone, I try not to leave my room; it's a confined space where I feel safe because there aren't any dangerous objects I

an unexpected MIRACLE

can hurt myself with. Even though I don't talk to a lot of people, I try to go out as much as possible; at least I'm in a different environment and I keep my mind occupied by looking around. I find that my mind calms down when I'm around people. When my mind is occupied on doing something constructive, I don't worry.

Besides the usual symptoms of anxiety and depression, I also experience situations of confusion, fatigue, and insomnia. I experience confusion when a person is talking to me and I can't follow what they're saying; I can't process their words quickly enough. Fatigue and insomnia go hand in hand. I get tired during the day either because I don't sleep properly at night or because my sleep is interrupted by flashbacks and I suddenly wake up and am not able to go back to sleep. Despite my worries and fears, I make every effort not to let these situations take over my life. I try to cope every way I can because I know that I have accomplished many things in life and I still have too much to look forward to. I think everything will play out once I feel accepted into society, when I make friends and build relationships with others (when?).

Maybe I don't have any friends because I tend to chase people away by not giving them their own space. The truth is I'm not trying to crowd them; I'm simply trying to help myself by reaching out to someone before my anxiety gets out of control. Many of you might not understand this because you've never gone through similar symptoms.

I know that I'm not the only person with anxiety in life. I acknowledge that life is hard for a typical individual: we're constantly faced with meeting the challenges of society. In this sense I'm no exception. But before making any assumptions, I would like YOU to fill my shoes for a day; you will see that my life isn't easy to live. In fact, life is twice as hard for me. I have to face the challenges of society as well as deal with my anxiety. You might ask yourself how I manage? Well, I guess I've developed the talent of distracting myself during the worst of times. I have a lot of strategies in place; I try to keep a positive mind, I exercise daily, I go shopping (or just look around), and yes, I constantly talk to a person once I get to know them. Just because I have issues with my anxiety doesn't mean I want to live in a bubble; I do not want to be isolated from society.

Chapter 7

I have feelings too

I am 26 years old and I have never been in a relationship with a man. But let's get one thing straight: I'm not a nun – I am attracted to men. At times I get depressed because too many years have gone by without having any kind of contact with men. I would imagine most people have gone through half a dozen boyfriends or are at least dating by the time they turn 26. *Why can't I have my share? Why is everybody so scared of me? Do I convey the wrong message to men? Do I have a negative body image?*

Growing up without a mother wasn't easy. Yeah, my dad remarried but my mother was irreplaceable. I know that my mother would have taught me about my womanhood and the changes my body would go through. I couldn't rely on my sister to teach me because she had a life of her own,

an unexpected MIRACLE

and my step-mom was out of the question. I had to teach myself, so I read up on the female reproductive system.

But on the rare occasion that I was able to talk to my step-mom or step-sister about sex, the conversations were awkward and brief. I used to feel like a nerd when anyone talked to me about sex because I usually didn't know how to answer them. I'd studied the biological side of it: they used slang terminology and words I couldn't understand. I felt so embarrassed. Therefore, I decided to take the situation into my own hands. I broadened my studies and read up on some non-scientific topics, gaining a broader knowledge about the reality of sex.

What is it (sex) like? How does it (sex) feel? I'll never know the definite answer until I experience it for myself. That said, I don't miss sex: how can I miss something I never tried? I don't know sex well enough to miss it. I want to have sex with the proper man; the man that will not take advantage of me. *When will the time come for me?*

I get why in high school I wasn't the most popular girl – kids can be really shallow at that age and I was definitely different – but I don't get why that same mentality seems to be continuing into my twenties. Do boys really take that long to grow up? Supposedly we're all grown up by the time we hit our mid-twenties. So why have men never approached me? Why do men see me differently?

Perhaps more than most women I'm really looking forward to meeting a man who can appreciate me for everything that I am, a man who has the maturity to love me and treat me with respect – a man who can understand that my brain injury is just an aspect of who I am, not the entirety. I don't know, maybe I'm still too young to move in the kind of crowd where men like that are found. Or maybe I'm not yet comfortable enough in public to really show off my awesome personality. Or, maybe

an unexpected MIRACLE

it's not my fault at all, and the men just haven't woken up to me yet.

I have the same desires, the same feelings, and the same fantasies as every other heterosexual female. Just because I have a brain injury doesn't mean that I don't want what other women want. I have feelings too; I want to be satisfied by a man too. In exchange, I know I have a lot to offer a man. I have a luscious body; I have a perfect figure that I work hard to keep. I am smart and caring, I have a big heart, and I am passionate. My physical appearance is completely normal; I'm not disfigured or missing a limb. Physically, I can do anything a woman should be able to do. Yes, gentlemen, anything.

Chapter 8

There is nothing to fear

Sometimes I think I need to more often ask people that question I once posed to Bill Roberts:

"Are you afraid of me?"

I'm a person like everyone else, with strengths and weaknesses, likes and dislikes, hopes and fears. Sure my voice is a little unusual, and it takes me longer to do certain things. But most "normal" people have some sort of permanent quirk and some skill they're not good at. One good quality I certainly have in spades, though, is determination.

I know I can succeed because I have the determination to do so. I always move forward, not backwards. I live life by two mottos: "nothing is impossible" and "never settle for less than your best."

I am living proof that nothing is impossible. My neurosurgeons didn't expect me to ever walk again;

an unexpected MIRACLE

they didn't expect me to ever talk again; they didn't expect me to regain my "smarts"; they didn't expect me to do a lot of things, but here I am today: walking, talking, full of smarts and living a full, independent life. Through no fault of my own my life took a wrong turn, but I fought hard to get back on life's road. Most people never get sent down a wrong turn like mine, and take their journey on life's road for granted. Not me. I fought for everything that I have, and I relish every day of my life. My eternal optimism, matched with my endless determination, might, I suppose, make me different from a "normal" person, but hopefully in a positive, inspiring way.

Never settle for less than your best: I don't. The Oxford Advanced Learner's Dictionary defines "best" as the most excellent type or quality. I do not stop until I get the best possible results. I always push myself a little harder than before. My sense of determination turns "I can't" into "I can," "I won't" into "I will," and "impossible" into "possible." Motivation drives me but determination keeps me going; it is the motor that turns my wheels.

Since the brutal day of the accident I have faced and overcome many obstacles. I faced and overcame the obstacle of eating solid food again; I faced and overcame the obstacle of using the toilet; I faced and overcame the obstacle of writing, of reading, of grooming myself.

Today I face a lot of invisible obstacles related to the psychological factors of the death of my mom. I have to assure myself that I will be okay without her by my side. For instance, I wake up every morning knowing that I have to take care of myself because my mom isn't here to lead the way. Venturing out on my own is an obstacle because I have to know the directions and reassure myself that I will be okay. The anxiety attacks I experience everyday are an obstacle because I have to find a way to calm myself.

an unexpected MIRACLE

I have come a long way on my journey but it's not over yet. My disabilities are becoming smaller and smaller the further I venture. I lost eight years of my life to rehab and I missed out on my childhood, but I do not grieve for my past. I am hungry for knowledge: this is my driver, my motivator, my determination.

And I know that all this drive can actually be scary for other people. Or at least it can make them uncomfortable. *Why does Jennifer push herself so hard? Why is she so focused on succeeding?* Maybe because everything in my life has been a challenge, and if I didn't push myself to my limits I wouldn't appear pretty much like a "normal" person today. I guess I could take it as a compliment that a casual observer gets uncomfortable at my determination to achieve something that might appear routine: maybe at a glance they think I'm just a "normal" person who shouldn't be worrying herself about that.

My determination is what's made me "normal." And I'm not going to stop here, no matter what other people might think.

What's the big deal about Jennifer being able to lift those weights? Why is she getting so excited about that song?

It's a big deal because a lot of experts once thought that I'd never be able to get out of bed, let alone lift weights. I'm excited about that song because a lot of experts once thought I'd never be able to make sense of sounds again.

All I want is to live a simple life; to enjoy what life has to offer. And I intend to keep pushing myself to find every joy that life has to offer. (Remember, gentlemen, I said anything.)

I don't dwell on my past; I use my past to inspire others to accomplish whatever they set their minds to. If I had a goal in mind, I had to be the one to initiate it; I couldn't wait for others to do it for me. Everything I wanted to accomplish had to start

an unexpected MIRACLE

with me. I had to have enough determination to go after what I wanted. My rehabilitation taught me how to do the basic skills needed for everyday life, but it was up to me to persevere, to perform a skill better than I was taught.

So, what exactly have I accomplished? How far was I able to go? Well, here's the answer... Today I can power walk and I can walk long distances. Sometimes my speech is slow but it has picked up a lot from the beginning; I have a wider vocabulary. I still tremble when I eat but I've learned proper etiquette at the dinner table. For my writing, I've learned to adapt by making use of a computer; my skills are clearly visible. I've long since overcome the "accidents" I had in bed, and now I wake myself up when the urge to go comes. My posture has improved; I'm walking taller with my shoulders back and my head up; I have more confidence. I am socializing more with others. My academic achievements speak for themselves: I received numerous awards throughout junior and senior high school. Every day is an improvement from yesterday. My journey isn't over yet—it has just begun.

So is there really anything to be afraid of? Nah. I'm just a regular lady trying to live her life as best as she can. I might still be a little afraid of you the first time we meet, but I'm working on that too.

Where do I see myself in ten or twenty years? This question is hard to answer, but I can tell you I will reach new limits.

The fitness field has really captured my interest. I guess the sparks lit up when I first started physiotherapy. Because I had to relearn to walk, I developed an appreciation for maintaining my fitness level and making sure that I never again lost the strength in my legs. These days I'm a member of the Fitness Inc. in Cranbrook. I spend a total workout time of one and a half to two hours which I split between cardio, weights, and socializing.

an unexpected MIRACLE

(There are other people at the gym, so why shouldn't I socialize?) I like the striding cardio machine as it helps me with my coordination, whereas the stationary bicycle helps me with my momentum. Both cardio exercises work my leg muscles, but they work my mind to help me walk more efficiently.

We walk with our brains, after all: our legs just respond to the message from our brains to put one foot in front of the other. It's the same for any other task; everything derives from our brains. I'll perform better if I have a healthy brain.

I started off slow on the weights, lifting only about five pounds, but today I can lift 15 to 30 pounds depending on the type of exercise. Whether I'm doing cardio or weight-lifting, I'm bringing oxygen to my brain which helps calm my anxiety and helps me think more clearly.

Physiotherapy only built my muscles enough, specifically my legs, to enable me to walk. Today,

Jennifer De Pippo

I've built up my shoulders, back, and arms as well. After months of hard work at the gym, my muscles gained strength and my body got toned. My intense dedication to engaging in an exercise routine has shown me what I can become. With a little hard work and a positive attitude I can exceed the average person. All I have to remember is that I will probably encounter more setbacks than achievements throughout my journey. When I experience a failure, I have to get back on my feet, learn from my mistake, and continue taking baby steps to get to where I want to be. Eventually, I will arrive. Things take time, they don't happen overnight.

Right now I'm pushing toward a new goal – maybe the most grandiose of my whole life. I'm training hard to be a competitive swimmer, and I've set as my goal nothing less than winning a medal for Canada at the Paralympics in Rio in 2016. Sound impossible? I don't really think so. Walking and

an unexpected MIRACLE

talking and living a regular life after suffering a contrecoup brain injury might sound impossible. Compared to how far I've come, Rio 2016 is just another milestone on my road of life.

That said, I'm taking this goal very seriously. I train seven days a week, between two and four hours a day, in the pool and the gym. I have to push through the fatigue and the pain like any athlete, but I also have to battle effects of my brain injury such as ataxia, where my muscles start to shake uncontrollably. My swim coach is proud of the progress I've made so far, and his support gives me even more determination to succeed, and I head to the pool on weekends when he's not with me, to practice my strokes and do drills on my own. But it's the words of my personal trainer in the gym that inspire me the most: "It's people like you, Jennifer, that make my job important." She sees the dedication that I have to succeed, and that in turn motivates her to push me and guide me even more.

Jennifer De Pippo

Eventually I'll have to settle down and get a real job, I suppose. Maybe one day I'll become a personal trainer or a fitness model, a sports therapist or a physiotherapist. Maybe even a wife to some wonderful man. The possibilities are endless. And I am not afraid to discover them. But for now, I'm going to live in this moment and enjoy it to the fullest: if you want to know where my life takes me, ask me in five, ten, or fifty years.

Appendix A

A bit about our brains

I decided to include a section in this book to educate my reader's on the brain. Let's face it – the three pound organ in our skulls is very complex. Our brain is made up entirely of **nerves** and floats in a fluid like substance. This fluid prevents our brain from banging on our skull when we move around therefore preventing any kind of injury. The skull acts as a helmet for our brain. Our brain is the control center for our entire body. Without our brain, we would be a mass of body parts without serving a purpose. Our brain sends signals to our **nerves** to certain parts of the body to make them work. All the qualities that define humanity derive from our brain. It is difficult to completely understand the brain because it is so powerful; it can do some unexpected things. Due to today's advanced technology, we are not only able to see the structure of the brain through **magnetic resonance imaging** but also how the brain develops and changes.

In the book called *The Brain Training Revolution: A Proven Workout For Healthy Brain Aging* by Paul E. Bendheim, M.D., states "the frontal lobe is responsible for making big decisions, planning, remembering long-term information and executing complex actions. When the frontal lobe is damaged, these tasks become a challenge…" The book goes on to state "The cerebellum is responsible for complex motor skills. When the cerebellum is damaged, muscle strength isn't lost, but fine coordination and motor control are…"

Another book, *The Brain That Changes Itself: Stories of Personal Triumph from the Frontiers of Brain Science* by Norman Doidge, M.D., states "The right hemisphere (of the brain) generally processes non-verbal communication; it allows us to recognize faces and read facial expressions, and it connects us to other people. The right hemisphere also processes the musical component of speech, or tone, by which we convey emotion. The left hemisphere generally processes the verbal-linguistic elements of speech, and analyzes problems using conscious processing." The book continues with "Babies have a larger right hemisphere, up to the end of the second year, and because the left hemisphere is only beginning its growth spurt,. their right hemisphere dominates the brain for the first three years of their lives. Twenty-six-month-olds are complex, "right-brained" emotional creatures but cannot talk about their experiences, a left-brain function. Brain scans show that during the first two years of life, the mother principally communicates nonverbally with her right hemisphere to reach her infant's right hemisphere."

Our brain, a mass of **neurons**, is the control system for all our body functions. When I fractured my

cranium (skull) I disrupted my **nervous** (both central (brain and spinal cord) and **peripheral** (dealing with the senses of touch, taste, smell, vision, hearing and balance)) **system**. Now I have trouble experiencing different body sensations. My **brain** has trouble sending the correct messages to different parts of my body.

A brain injury can either be focal – confined to one area of the brain – or diffuse – involving multiple areas of the brain. A brain injury can result from either a **penetrating head injury** or a **closed head injury**. A **closed head injury** occurs when the head spontaneously hits an object with maximum force but the object does not break through the skull; hence the term "closed"; the skull is still intact. A **penetrating head injury** occurs when an object pierces through the skull and penetrates brain tissue. Several different types of brain injuries exist.

Skull fractures are vulnerable to head injuries and occur when the bone of the skull cracks or breaks. A

depressed skull fracture occurs when pieces of the broken skull penetrate the tissue of the brain whereas a **penetrating skull fracture** occurs when an object penetrates the skull itself, such as a bullet, injuring the surrounding brain tissue.

Skull fractures can cause bruising of brain tissue called a **contusion**; a distinct area of swollen brain tissue mixed with blood released from broken blood vessels. A **contusion** can also occur in response to shaking of the brain back and forth within the confines of the skull; called a **countercoup**. A **countercoup** often occurs in car accidents and shaken baby syndrome. **Countercoup** (what my brain injury is called) can cause diffuse axonal injury, damage to individual nerve cells (neurons) and loss of connections among **neurons**. Damage to a major blood vessel in the head can cause a **hematoma** (heavy bleeding into or around the brain). There are three types of hematomas that can cause brain damage. An **epidural hematoma** involves bleeding into the area between the skull and the **dura**. In a **subdural hematoma**, bleeding is confined to the area between the **dura** and the **arachnoid membrane**. Bleeding within the brain is called **intracerebral hematoma** (what I experienced).

A brain injury can cause problems for the individual with arousal, **consciousness**, awareness, alertness, and responsiveness. There are five states of consciousness that can result from a brain injury: **stupor, coma, persistent vegetative state, locked-in syndrome**, and **brain death**.

Stupor is a state where the patient is unresponsive but can suddenly be aroused by a strong stimulus, such as sharp pain. **Coma** is a state where the patient is totally unconscious, unaware, unresponsive, and unarousable. Patients do not respond to external stimuli and do not have sleep-wake cycles. **Coma** results from widespread and diffuse trauma to the brain. A **coma** can last anywhere from a few days to a few weeks after which time patients progress to a **vegetative state** or die if they do not come out of the **coma**.

Patients in a **vegetative state** are unconscious and unaware of their surroundings, but can experience sleep-wake cycles and periods of alertness. In a **vegetative state**, patients usually open their eyes and may move, groan, or show reflex responses. This state results from diffuse injury to the hemispheres of the brain. Many patients emerge from a **vegetative state** within a few weeks. If patients do not recover within 30 days are said to be in a **pervasive vegetative state (PVS)**.

Locked-in syndrome is caused by damage to specific portions of the lower brain and brain stem with no damage to the upper brain. Most of these patients can communicate through movements and blinking their eyes. Some patients may have the ability to move certain facial muscles, but the majority of patients do not regain motor control due to **paralysis** of the body. Moreover, **brain death** is the lack of measurable brain function due to diffuse damage to the brain with loss of any integrated activity. **Brain death** is irreversible.

Our brain has the ability to restructure and heal itself overtime; our brain is not ridged and hardwired; it is plastic. The brain has the ability to "reroute" itself when performing a regular routine would be hard using the regular way would be hard due to injury. The same results are achieved but (it) will take somewhat longer to complete. This is known as **neuroplasticity**. New **neurons** are always developing in our brains especially in the learning and memory centers. When you become an expert in a skill, the corresponding areas in the brain of the skill grow. In addition, when **neurons** activate at the same time as a response to an event, the **neurons** become associated with one another and the connections become stronger. However, if not utilized, the **neurons** will be used for another response; hence the phrase *"use it or lose it"*.

Our brains are made up of six different parts: the **Frontal Lobe, Temporal Lobe, Occipital Lobe, Parietal Lobe, Cerebellum,** and **Brain Stem**. These parts appear in both hemispheres and each carry out their own functions. The **Frontal Lobes** are located right under the forehead and carries out functions such as our **consciousness**, how we initiate activity in response to our environment, the judgments we make about what occurs in our daily activities, emotional response, expressive language, assigning meaning to the words we choose, word associations, and memory for our habits and motor skills/activities. The **Parietal Lobes** are located near the back and top of the head. It's functions include the location of visual attention, the location of touch perception, goal directed voluntary movements, manipulation of objects, and the integration of different senses that allows for understanding a concept. The **Occipital Lobes** are located at the back rear of the head. The main purpose of the Occipital Lobes is vision. *We see with our brains. Our eyes simply reflect the image.* The **Temporal Lobes** are located on opposite sides of the head above the ears. These lobes are responsible for hearing ability, memory acquisition, visual perceptions, and categorization of objects. The **Brain Stem** lies deep within the brain and leads to the spinal cord, and is responsible for our **startle response, autonomic nervous system, vestibular function**, level of alertness, and ability to sleep. The **Cerebellum** is located at the base of the skull. It carries out the coordination of voluntary movements of balance and equilibrium and some memory for reflex motor acts.

When a brain injury occurs, the brain may be injured in a specific area or may be diffused throughout the brain. Knowing the nature of the brain can enable **rehabilitation** specialists to make approximate hypothesizes about the nature of the problems an individual may have if the location of the wound is known. **Diagnostic imaging** such as **computed tomography scans (CT scans)** and **magnetic resonance imagings (MRI's)** help to better understand a **brain injury**. But, by observing the day to day activities of the patient, **rehabilitation** specialists can learn about the patient's injury because the mental and physical activities we perform each day are directed by different parts of the **brain**. It is very important to understand that the **rehabilitation** professional is concerned with the whole person. Each problem area affects other areas and many times resolving one problem has a major impact on other problems. Reestablishing postural balance and eliminating dizziness enhances concentration and attention which allows for improved cognition and problem solving.

When the **Frontal Lobes** get injured, we experience **paralysis, sequencing, preservation, attending, emotional labile, Broca's aphasia,** loss of spontaneity in interacting with others, loss of flexibility in thinking, changes in social behavior, changes in personality, and difficulty with problem solving. Injury to the **Parietal Lobes** result in the inability to attend to more than one object at a time, **anomia, agraphia, alexia,** difficulty with drawing objects, difficulty in distinguishing left from right, **dyscalculia, apraxia,** inability to focus visual attention, and difficulties with eye-hand coordination. Injury to the **Occipital Lobes** result in **visual field cuts,** difficulty with locating objects in the environment, **color agnosia,** hallucinating, visual illusions, inaccurately seeing objects, word blindness, difficulty in recognizing drawn objects, **movement agnosia,** and difficulties with reading and writing. Injury to the **Temporal Lobes** result in **prosopagnosia, Wernicke's aphasia,** disturbance with selective attention to what is seen and heard, difficulty with identification of and verbalization about objects, short-term memory loss, interference with long-term memory, increased or decreased interest in sexual behavior, and **categorization**. Damage to the right lobe of the **Temporal Lobes** can cause persistent talking and increased aggressive behavior. Problems associated with injury to the **Brain Stem** include **dysphagia**, organization and perception of the environment, balance and movement, **vertigo, insomnia,** and **sleep apnea**. Damage to the **cerebellum** result in the loss of the ability to coordinate fine movements, loss of the ability to walk, inability to reach out and grab objects, tremors, **vertigo, scanning speech**, and the inability to make rapid movements.

Other parts of the body are commonly injured when suffering from a brain injury. This term is known as **polytrauma**. Some complications that may accompany a brain injury include **pulmonary**

dysfunction, **cardiovascular dysfunction** from chest trauma, **gastrointestinal dysfunction**, fluid and hormonal imbalances, and other isolated complications, such as fractures, nerve injuries, **deep vein thrombosis**, excessive blood clotting, and infections.

Appendix B

Medical Terminology Associated with a Brian Injury

agraphia: inability to locate the words for writing

alexia: problems with reading

anomia: inability to name an object

anoxia: an absence of oxygen supply to an organ's tissues leading to cell death

apraxia: lack of awareness of certain body parts and/or surrounding space. This typically leads to difficulties in self-care

arachnoid membrane: one of the three membranes that cover the brain; it is between the pia mater and the dura

ataxia: failure of muscular coordination; irregularity of muscular action

attending: inability to focus on a task

audio therapy: therapy that teaches deaf and hard of hearing children to listen and speak using their hearing and hearing devices, such as hearing aids, FM systems (a device that enables a person to control the loudness of the voice of the person talking to you), and cochlear implants (sound transmitted through the brain)

autonomic nervous system: function that controls bodily functions such as breathing, heart rate, blood pressure, digestion, sweating and body temperature

bilateral coordination: the ability to use both sides of the body at the same time. This can mean using the two sides for the same action (like using a rolling pin) or using alternating movements (like climbing stairs)

brain: an organ in the head that acts as a control center for the whole body

brain death: an irreversible cessation of measurable brain function

brain injury: a bump, blow, or jolt that causes damage to the brain

brain stem: implemented deep within the brain and leads to the spinal cord.

Broca's Aphasia: impairment of expressing language

cardiovascular dysfunction: improper functioning of the heart and blood vessels

categorization: Inability to categorize objects

central nervous system: composed of the brain and spinal cord; the main "processing center" for the entire nervous system; and controls all the workings of your body

Cerebellum: the part of the brain located at the base of the skull

closed head injury: an injury that occurs when the head suddenly and violently hits an object but the object does not break through the skull

cognition: the mental process of knowing, including aspects such as awareness, perception, reasoning, and judgment

cognitive: of pertaining to the act or process of knowing, perceiving, and remembering

color agnosia: difficulty identifying colors

coma: a deep sleep; a state of extreme unresponsiveness in which an individual exhibits no voluntary movement or behavior. In a deep coma, even painful stimuli (actions which, when performed on a healthy individual, result in reactions) are unable to affect any response, and normal reflexes may be lost

computed tomography scans (CT scans): a medical imaging method that employs the process of generating a two-dimensional image through a three-dimensional object

concussion: injury to the brain caused by a hard blow or violent shaking, causing a sudden and temporary impairment of brain function, such as a short loss of consciousness or disturbance of vision and equilibrium

conscious: aware of one's own existence, sensations, thoughts, surroundings, etc

consciousness: how we know what we are doing in our environment

contrecoup: a contusion caused by the shaking of the brain back and forth within the confines of the skull

contusion: distinct area of swollen brain tissue mixed with blood released from broken blood vessels

coordination: the ability to control your movements well

cranium: the portion of the skull enclosing the brain; the braincase

deep vein thrombosis: formation of a blood clot deep within a vein

depressed skull fracture: a fracture occuring when pieces of broken skull press into the tissues of the brain

dexterity: skill in using the hands

diagnostic imaging: a form of medical imaging that is performed with the intention of finding a disease, or to monitor the progress of a disease, or to guide a medical procedure

dura: a tough, fibrous membrane lining the brain; the outermost of the three membranes

dysarthria: when you have difficulty saying words because of problems with the muscles that help you talk.

dyscalculia: difficulty doing mathematics

dysphalgia: difficulty in swallowing

emotionally labile: mood changes

epidural hematoma: bleeding into the area between the skull and the dura

equilibrium: balance

frontal lobes: the area occupying the front part of the brain; it is right under the forehead

functional magnetic resonance imaging (fMRI): an MRI procedure that measures brain activity by detecting associated changes in blood flow

gastrointestinal dysfunction: problems associated with the stomach and intestines

general anesthesia: a medically induced coma and loss of protective reflexes. The purposes of general anesthesia are loss of response to pain, loss of memory, loss of motor reflexes, loss of consciousness, and skeletal muscle relaxation

Glasgow Coma Score: one of the tools doctors use to determine how serious a brain injury is. The scale is composed of three parameters and is scored from 3 to 15; 3 being a severe brain injury

grading: giving a value to a clinical sign so that its relative importance in the diagnosis of a particular disease is given its appropriate wieghing, a matter of some significance in computer-assisted diagnoses. The numerical value for a particular clinical sign may very well vary widely for different diseases

hematoma: heavy bleeding into or around the brain caused by damage to a major blood vessel in the head

hypoxia: decreased oxygen levels in an organ

impairment: any abnormality of, partial or complete loss of, or loss of the function of, a body part, organ, or system

insomnia: inability/difficulty to sleep

intracerebral hematoma: bleeding within the brain caused by damage to a major blood vessel

intracranial pressure: buildup of pressure in the brain as a result of injury

kyphosis: extreme curvature of the upper back also known as a hunchback

left-brained: relating to a person whose behavior is dominanted by logic, analytical thinking, and verbal communication, rather than emotion and creativity

lexical access: an aspect of cognitive psychology that looks at the variables that affect word choice and word recognition from an individual's lexicon

lexicon: the vocabulary of a particular language, field, social class, person, etc

locked-in syndrome: a condition in which a patient is aware and awake, but cannot move or communicate due to complete paralysis of the body.

magnetic resonance imaging (MRI): used in radiology to visualize internal structures of the body in detail

movement agnosia: inability to recognize the movement of an object

nervous system: the network of specialized cells, tissues, and organs in a multicellular animal that coordinates the body's interaction with the environment, including sensing internal and external stimuli, monitoring the organs, coordinating the activity of muscles, initiating actions, and regulating behavior

nerve: fibers that convey impulses (send messages) between different parts of the body; how the body communicates

neurologist: a physician specializing in neurology and trained to investigate, or diagnose and treat neurological disorders

neurology: a medical specialty dealing with disorders of the nervous system

neuron: cell that processes and transmits information through electrical and chemical signals; the brain is made up entirely of neurons

neuroplasticity: the brain's ability to reorganize itself by forming new neural connections throughout life

neuropsychologist: a person who studies the effects of brain damage on behavior and the mind

neuroscience: the scientific study of the nervous system in all of its aspects

neurosurgeons: the surgical procedure of neurology

occipital lobes: the part of the brain at the back of the head

occupational therapist: a person who works with a client to help them achieve a fulfilled and satisfied state in life through the use of "purposeful activity or interventions designed to achieve functional outcomes which promote health, prevent injury or disability and which develop, improve, sustain, or restore the highest possible level of independence

paralysis: loss of simple movements of various body parts

parietal lobes: the part of the brain near the back and top part of the head

penetrating head injury: a brain injury in which an object pierces the skull and enters the brain tissue

penetrating skull fracture: a brain injury in which an object pierces the skull and injures brain tissue

peripheral nervous system: all elements of the nevous system outside the brain and spinal cord; referring to the senses of touch, taste, smell, vision, and hearing

perseveration: persistence of a single thought

persistent vegetative state: an ongoing state of severely impaired consciousness in which the patient is incapable of voluntary motion

physiotherapist: a person referred to as a "movement specialist". Therapists are trained to access and treat a variety of conditions that affect the physical functions of an individual

polytrauma: the occurrence of injuries to more than one body system

prosopagnosia: difficulty in recognizing faces

pulmonary dysfunction: insufficient lung capacity

rehabilitation a treatment or treatments designed to facilitate the process of recovery from injury, illness, or disease to as normal a condition as possible

rehabilitation: includes assisting the patient to compensate for deficits that cannot be reversed medically

right brained: relating to a person whose behavior is dominant by emotion, creativity, intuition, non-verbal communication, and global reasoning rather than logic and analysis

rules of pragmatics:

    1) taking turns in conversation

    2) introducing topics of conversation

    3) staying on topic

    4) rephrasing when misunderstood

    5) how to use verbal and non-verbal signals

    6) how close to stand to someone when speaking

    7) how to use facial expression and eye contact

salience stimulus: the state or quality by which an item stands out relative to its neighbors

scanning speech: slurred speech

sequencing: inability of completing the steps taken to complete a task, such as making coffee

sleep apnea: inability/difficulty to sleep due to forced breathing

speech therapist: a person who specializes in communication and swallowing disorders

speech therapy: treatment of speech defects and disorders, especially through exercises and the use of audio-visual aids

stabilized: to intervene in a critically ill patient to minimize the possibility of acute decompensation of vital functions.

startle response: reflexes to seeing and hearing

stupor: a state of impaired consciousness in which the patient is unresponsive but can be aroused briefly by a strong stimulus

subdural hematoma: bleeding confined to the area between the dura and the arachnoid membranes

temporal lobes: the part of the brain on the sides of the head above the ears

utterance: the smallest unit of speech

vegetative state: a condition in which patients are unconscious and unaware of their surroundings but continue to have a sleep/wake cycle and can have periods of alertness

vertigo: dizziness and nausea

vestibular function: sense of balance and equilibrium

visual field cuts: defects in vision

visual-motor control: use of visual information to perform smooth, coordinated, and precise movements

visual-perceptual: the ability to interpret the surrounding environment by processing information that is contained in visible light

visual-spatial: of or relating to visual perception of spatial relationships among objects; the skills needed to complete a jigsaw puzzle

Wernicke's aphasia: difficulty in understanding spoken words

word blindness: inability to recognize words

About the author

Jennifer is 26 years old and resides in Cranbrook, British Columbia, Canada with her father and stepmother. She decided to write this book to inspire people to never give up hope. Anything is possible if you believe.